One Hand, One Heart

FROM

WEST SIDE STORY®

Music by

Leonard Bernstein®

Lyrics by

Stephen Sondheim

LEONARD
BERNSTEIN
Music Publishing
Company LLC

BOOSEY & HAWKES

DISTRIBUTED BY

HAL•LEONARD®

One Hand, One Heart

from *West Side Story*

original key

Lyrics by
STEPHEN SONDHEIM

Music by
LEONARD BERNSTEIN

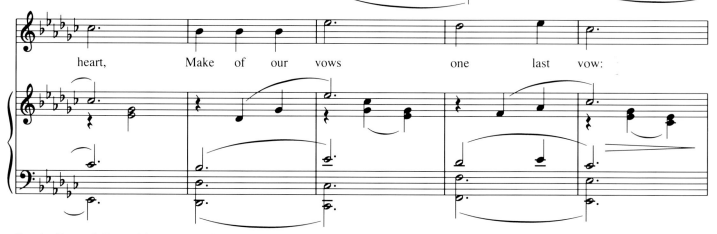

See the Duets & Ensembles volume of *Bernstein Theatre Songs* for the original duet version for Maria and Tony.
Adapted as a solo for this edition.

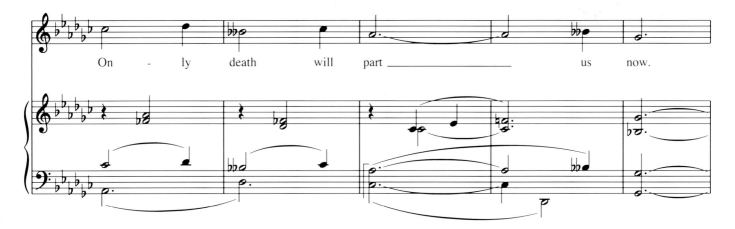

On - ly death will part _____ us now.

Make of our lives one life,

p dolce

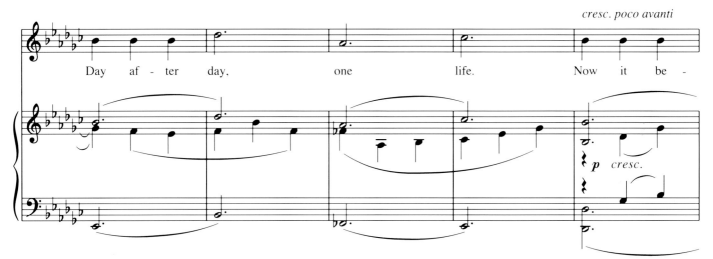

cresc. poco avanti

Day af - ter day, one life. Now it be -

p cresc.

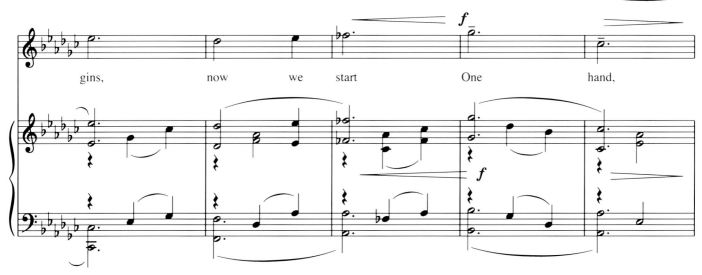

f

gins, now we start One hand,

f

one heart; E - ven death won't part us now.

Make of our lives one

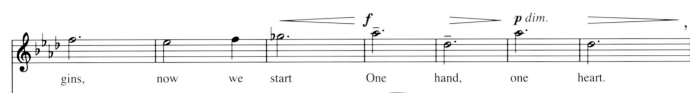

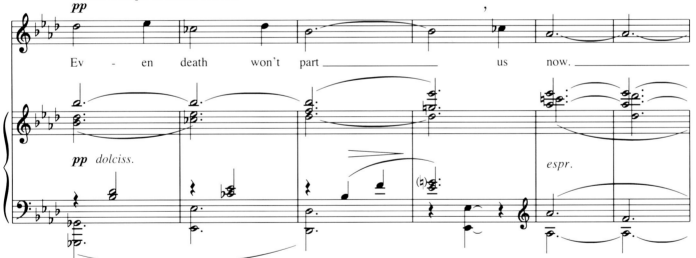

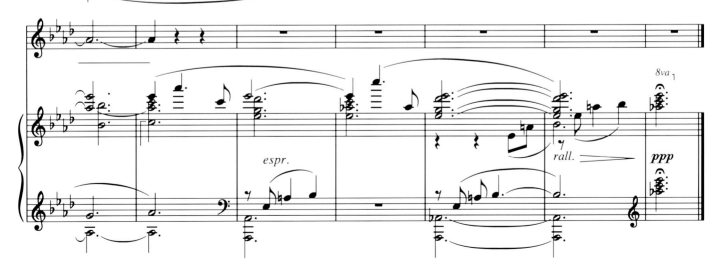

ABOUT THE ENHANCED CD

In addition to piano accompaniments playable on both your CD player and computer, this enhanced CD also includes tempo adjustment and transposition software for computer use only. This software, known as Amazing Slow Downer, was originally created for use in pop music to allow singers and players the freedom to independently adjust both tempo and pitch elements. Because we believe there may be valuable educational use for these features in classical and theatre music, we have included this software as a tool for both the teacher and student. For quick and easy installation instructions of this software, please see below.

In recording a piano accompaniment we necessarily must choose one tempo. Our choice of tempo, phrasing, ritardandos, and dynamics is carefully considered. But by the nature of recording, it is only one option.

However, we encourage you to explore your own interpretive ideas, which may differ from our recordings. This new software feature allows you to adjust the tempo up and down without affecting the pitch. Likewise, Amazing Slow Downer allows you to shift pitch up and down without affecting the tempo. We recommend that these new tempo and pitch adjustment features be used with care and insight. Ideally, you will be using these recorded accompaniments and Amazing Slow Downer for practice only.

The audio quality may be somewhat compromised when played through the Amazing Slow Downer. This compromise in quality will not be a factor in playing the CD audio track on a normal CD player or through another audio computer program.

INSTALLATION INSTRUCTIONS:

For Macintosh OS 8, 9 and X:
- Load the CD-ROM into your CD-ROM Drive on your computer.
- Each computer is set up a little differently. Your computer may automatically open the audio CD portion of this enhanced CD and begin to play it.
- To access the CD-ROM features, double-click on the data portion of the CD-ROM (which will have the Hal Leonard icon in red and be named as the book).
- Double-click on the "Amazing OS 8 (9 or X)" folder.
- Double-click "Amazing Slow Downer"/"Amazing X PA" to run the software from the CD-ROM, or copy this file to your hard disk and run it from there.
- Follow the instructions on-screen to get started. The Amazing Slow Downer should display tempo, pitch and mix bars. Click to select your track and adjust pitch or tempo by sliding the appropriate bar to the left or to the right.

For Windows:
- Load the CD-ROM into your CD-ROM Drive on your computer.
- Each computer is set up a little differently. Your computer may automatically open the audio CD portion of this enhanced CD and begin to play it.
- To access the CD-ROM features, click on My Computer then right click on the Drive that you placed the CD in. Click Open. You should then see a folder named "Amazing Slow Downer". Click to open the "Amazing Slow Downer" folder.
- Double-click "setup.exe" to install the software from the CD-ROM to your hard disk. Follow the on-screen instructions to complete installation.
- Go to "Start," "Programs" and find the "Amazing Slow Downer" folder. Go to that folder and select the "Amazing Slow Downer" software.
- Follow the instructions on-screen to get started. The Amazing Slow Downer should display tempo, pitch and mix bars. Click to select your track and adjust pitch or tempo by sliding the appropriate bar to the left or to the right.
- Note: On Windows NT, 2000, XP, Vista, and 7, the user should be logged in as the "Administrator" to guarantee access to the CD-ROM drive. Please see the help file for further information.

MINIMUM SYSTEM REQUIREMENTS:

For Macintosh:
Power Macintosh; Mac OS 8.5 or higher, OSX; 4 MB Application RAM; 8x Multi-Session CD-ROM drive

For Windows:
Pentium, Celeron or equivalent processor; Windows 95, 98, ME, NT, 2000, XP, Vista, 7; 4 MB Application RAM; 8x Multi-Session CD-ROM drive